Trot, Pony!

Shira Evans

NATIONAL GEOGRAPHIC

Washington, D.C.

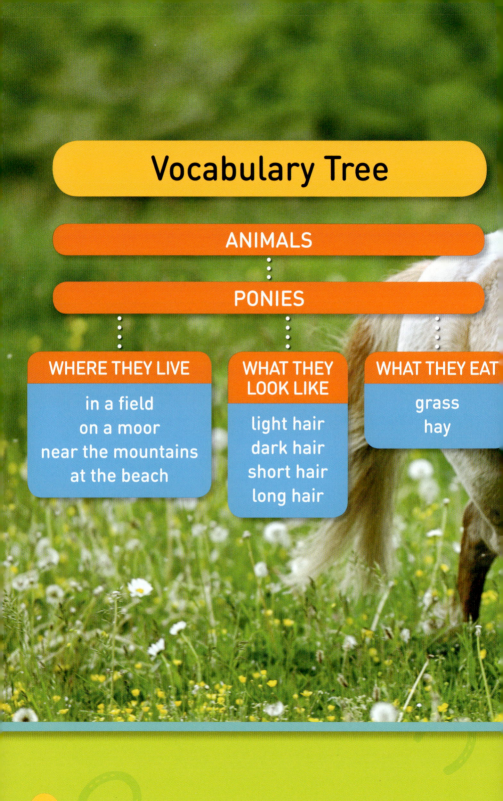

These young ponies play.

They live in a field.

Exmoor ponies

Dartmoor ponies

These ponies live on a moor.

It's grassy and hilly here.

Ponies live in a group called a herd.

Icelandic horses

This herd lives near the mountains.

This herd lives at the beach.

Chincoteague ponies

There are ponies with light hair.

Welsh pony

Exmoor pony

There are ponies with dark hair.

Some ponies have short hair.

Haflinger pony

Shetland pony

Some ponies have long hair.

All ponies eat grass.

Norwegian fjord horse

Welsh pony

They eat hay, too.

Shetland ponies

Play, ponies!

Trot, pony!

Shetland pony

Kinds of Ponies

There are many kinds of ponies. These are the kinds in this book.

ICELANDIC HORSE

WELSH MOUNTAIN PONY

EXMOOR PONY

DARTMOOR PONY

CHINCOTEAGUE PONY

WELSH PONY

HAFLINGER PONY

SHETLAND PONY

NORWEGIAN FJORD HORSE

YOUR TURN!

Draw a pony! Say what it looks like.

light hair
dark hair
short hair
long hair

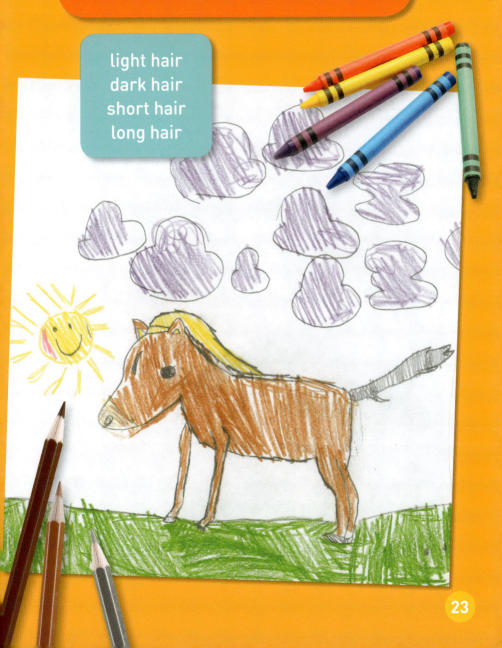

Copyright © 2016 National Geographic Partners, LLC

Published by National Geographic Partners, LLC, Washington, D.C. 20036. All rights reserved. Reproduction of the whole or any part of the contents without written permission from the publisher is prohibited.

Library of Congress Cataloging-in-Publication Data

Names: Evans, Shira, author.
Title: Trot, pony! / by Shira Evans.
Description: Washington, DC : National Geographic, [2016] | Series: National Geographic readers | Audience: Ages 2-5.
Identifiers: LCCN 2015041576| ISBN 9781426324130 (pbk. : alk. paper) | ISBN 9781426324147 (library binding : alk. paper)
Subjects: LCSH: Wild ponies--Behavior--Juvenile literature. | Wild ponies--Juvenile literature. | Ponies--Juvenile literature.
Classification: LCC SF315 .E83 2016 | DDC 599.665/5--dc23

The publisher gratefully acknowledges the expert literacy review of this book by Susan B. Neuman, Ph.D., professor of early childhood and literacy education, New York University.

Designed by Callie Broaddus

Photo Credits

Cover, Juniors Bildarchiv GmbH/Alamy; 1 (CTR), Juniors Bildarchiv GmbH/Alamy; 2-3 (CTR), Juniors Bildarchiv GmbH/Alamy; 4-5 (CTR), Wildlife GmbH/Alamy; 6-7 (CTR), David Lyons/Alamy; 8-9 (CTR), Ratnakorn Piyasirisorost/Getty Images; 10-11 (CTR), Stephen Bonk/Shutterstock; 12 (CTR), Juniors Bildarchiv GmbH/Alamy; 13 (CTR), Adam Burton/robertharding/Corbis; 14 (CTR), Katho Menden/Shutterstock; 15 (CTR), Juniors Bildarchiv GmbH/Alamy; 16 (CTR), Foto Grebler/Alamy; 17 (CTR), Groomes Photography/Getty Images; 18-19 (CTR), Juniors Bildarchiv GmbH/Alamy; 20-21 (CTR), Sabine Stuewer/KimballStock; 22 (UP LE), kb-photodesign/Shutterstock; 22 (CTR LE), Nicole Ciscato/Shutterstock; 22 (LO LE), Peak District Ventures/Getty Images; 22 (UP CTR), Zuzule/Shutterstock; 22 (CTR), Robert Kirk/Getty Images; 22 (LO CTR), David & Micha Sheldon/Getty Images; 22 (UP RT), Mike Charles/Shutterstock; 22 (CTR RT), Martyn Barnwell/Alamy; 22 (LO RT), David Robertson/Alamy; 23 (UP RT), Bogdan Ionescu/Shutterstock; 23 (CTR), Kaya Dengel; 23 (LO LE), Lukas Gojda/Shutterstock; 24 (UP), Juniors Bildarchiv GmbH/Alamy

National Geographic supports K–12 educators with ELA Common Core Resources. Visit natgeoed.org/commoncore for more information.

Printed in the United States of America
21/WOR/4